HURRICANE HARVEY

Donald Gorbach

ISBN-10 1979392943
ISBN-13 978-1979392945

"COME TO MY OFFICE.
I WANT TO MAKE MOVIES WITH YOU.
I CAN MAKE YOU A STAR."

—HARVEY WEINSTEIN